CARD TRICKS

STEPHANIE TURNBULL

A+

Smart Apple Media

Published by Smart Apple Media
P.O. Box 3263
Mankato, MN 56002

Printed in the United States of America at Corporate Graphics,
in North Mankato, Minnesota.

Library of Congress Cataloging-in-Publication Data
Turnbull, Stephanie.
  Card tricks / Stephanie Turnbull.
      p. cm. -- (Secrets of magic)
  Includes index.
  ISBN 978-1-59920-495-6 (library binding)
  1. Card tricks--Juvenile literature. I. Title.
  GV1549.T85 2012
  793.8'5--dc22

                          2010035667

Created by Appleseed Editions, Ltd.
Designed and illustrated by Guy Callaby
Edited by Mary-Jane Wilkins
Picture research by Su Alexander

Picture credits:
t = top, b = bottom
Contents page and pages 4,6 & 8t Shutterstock, 8b JoeFoxPhoto/Alamy;
10 Stephen Wilson Photography/Alamy; 12, 14, 16, 18t & 20 Shutterstock;
22 Jason Harowitz/Alamy; 24t Shutterstock, b WireIMAGE/Getty; 27 Jennifer Brown/
Star Ledger/Corbis; 28 The Protected Art Archive/Alamy; 29 Shutterstock
Front cover: Gelpi/Shutterstock

DAD0049
3-2011

9 8 7 6 5 4 3 2 1

Contents

Pick a Card...

IF YOU WANT to become a magician, then card tricks are the perfect way to start. A deck of cards is cheap, fits easily in your pocket or bag, and can be whipped out at any time to give your friends a taste of your skills! Card magic has been around for hundreds of years and there are all kinds of tricks to try.

Early card tricks were often played in the street, and many still are today. A dealer invites passers-by to bet on certain cards—then cheats to make sure they never win.

THE OLDEST TRICK?

The first card tricks were invented to cheat people out of money in card games. Perhaps the oldest card trick of all is Three Card Monte, which is usually played in the street. A **dealer** shows someone three cards—usually a queen and two jacks —then puts them face down and mixes them up. The person tries to win money by betting on which one is the queen. The dealer uses false deals and clever flips, changing the cards around, so the person never chooses the queen. You can learn some dealing tricks on pages 20–21.

S. W. ERDNASE (18??–19??)

In 1902 a book appeared in America called The Expert at the Card Table by S. W. Erdnase. It revealed many of the tricks used by card cheats and is the most famous book of card tricks ever written. You can still buy it today. But no one called S. W. Erdnase ever existed. So who wrote the book?

If you spell S. W. Erdnase backwards, you get E. S. Andrews, the name of a **con man** who lived around the same time the book appeared. He cheated a lot of businessmen out of money, went to jail and later disappeared. Could he have written the book to make money? Some people think the author was W. E. Sanders, a rich engineer whose name is an **anagram** of S. W. Erdnase. Or perhaps it was another con man called M. F. Andrews? We may never know the answer.

TRICK TYPES

There are two types of card magic: self-working tricks and **sleight-of-hand** tricks. To perform self-working tricks you stack or deal the cards so the trick works automatically. You don't need special skills, but the tricks do need lots of practice so you remember exactly what to do. Sleight-of-hand tricks ("sleights" for short) use secret moves and are harder to learn. Many take years to perfect—but if you do them right, they look amazing!

Now you see it . . .

. . . now you don't!

Go to pages 26 and 27 to find out how to do sleight-of-hand tricks.

TRICK OF THE TRADE
The tricks in this book are all described for right-handed people, so if you're left-handed you'll have to swap the words "left" and "right" —or try them both ways and see which works best for you.

Tricks of the Trade

IF YOU WANT to become a card expert, there are three Ps to remember. The first is Practice. Practicing hard is the only way to master tricks. Never waste a trick by showing it before you can do it perfectly, as you may give away the secret. Once you know what you're doing without thinking about it, you can work on the other Ps: Patter and Performance.

PERFECT PATTER

Patter is what you say while doing a trick. It helps to keep your audience entertained, but it's also essential to direct people's attention away from things you don't want them to notice. For instance, you might ask them to inspect one card while secretly moving another. You can also use patter to make certain things clear to the audience (for example, reminding them that you let your volunteer choose *any* card) or to make the climax of a trick more impressive.

Props such as a hat or wand can help to distract the audience. For example, while you wave your wand dramatically or ask people to check that your hat is empty, you could be sneaking something out of your pocket.

POLISHED PERFORMANCE

The way you perform your trick is as important as the trick itself. Without a good performance, even a perfect trick can fall flat. Like patter, the way you perform keeps everyone interested, but also helps to **misdirect** their attention when you want to. Turn to pages 28–29 for performance tips.

THE FLYING CARD

Try this small trick to test your performing confidence and your ability to misdirect people's attention. They will soon figure out what you've done, but for a moment you might have them fooled—and that's what tricks are all about. Just don't forget to practice it first.

TRICK OF THE TRADE
Film yourself to see what your performance looks like. It's easier than trying to watch yourself in a mirror!

1. When you're sitting at a table with friends, hold up a card and announce that you're going to make it fly away. Hold the card as if you're about to throw it.

2. Look where the card would go if you did throw it, drop it in your lap and whip your hand in the direction you're looking. If you do this quickly and confidently, everyone will look to see where the card went.

The card is in your lap.

MASTER MAGICIAN

ED MARLO (1913–1991)

Ed Marlo is one of the world's most famous card magicians. He wrote more than 60 books on card magic and invented around 2,000 tricks. These ranged from simple, self-working effects to very difficult shuffling methods. He created the term "cardician" to describe a magician who only performs card tricks. The secret of his success was constant, obsessive practice. He took a deck of cards with him everywhere. Once, some friends arranged a birthday meal for Marlo, but he didn't turn up. Eventually his friends found him in his car, completely absorbed in figuring out a new trick.

Getting Started

THE GREAT THING about card tricks is that you don't need expensive or complicated equipment—just a deck of cards. Buy a good quality deck with a plastic coating, as this makes the cards smooth and easier to **shuffle**. If any cards get torn or bent, don't throw the pack away. Keep it to practice with.

Know Your Cards

There are 52 cards in an ordinary deck, divided into four suits. These are usually hearts, diamonds, spades, and clubs, although this can vary in different countries. There are also two or four **jokers**. Unless your trick needs them, take the jokers out of the deck before you begin.

Buy cards with a white space around the edge on the back. This may be useful if you need to pretend that cards are face-down . . .

. . . when really they're face-up.

Special Cards

You can buy all kinds of cards for tricks, including giant cards that are easy to see, cards with two backs or two faces, and cards with shaved edges that make them easy for you to pick out in a regular deck. The problem is that you can only use them in a few tricks, so they may not be worth buying—especially since there are so many tricks you can do with ordinary cards.

Giant cards are easy to see but hard to shuffle!

JOHANN NEPOMUK HOFZINSER (1806–1875)

Hofzinser was an Austrian magician who is often called "The Father of Card Magic." In 1857, he and his wife began inviting rich and important guests to their home in Vienna to watch illusions and card tricks. The shows were a big success, and Hofzinser later performed all around Europe. He was one of the first performers to use cards as part of a magic act, rather than as a way of cheating in card games. As well as inventing many sleight-of-hand moves, he also used specially-made trick cards; for example, he had cards with one design on the top half and a different design on the bottom half.

DEAL AND DOUBLE DEAL

Here's a simple and effective trick to help you get used to your cards.

1. Ask a friend to pull out all the cards of one suit and put them in order from lowest to highest: ace (1), 2, 3, 4, 5, 6, 7, 8, 9, 10, jack, queen, king. Put the rest of the deck to one side.

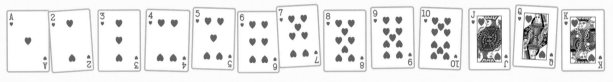

2. Tell your friend you're going to deal out his cards and you want him to help mix them up. When he says, "Deal," you deal one card face down on the table. When he says, "Double deal," you switch the order of the next two cards before dealing them both together.

3. When all the cards are dealt, say, "Let's see how well you mixed them up." Turn the cards over and spread them out. They are still in order!

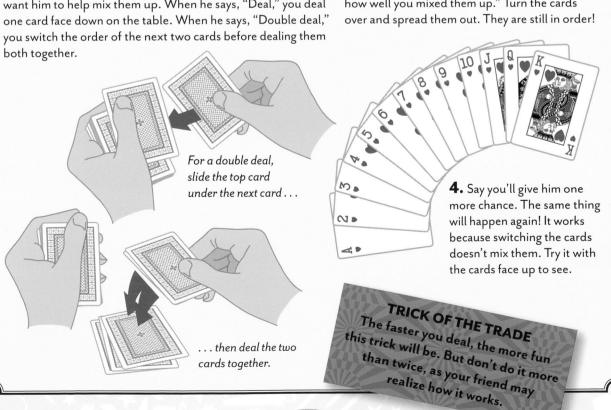

For a double deal, slide the top card under the next card . . .

. . . then deal the two cards together.

4. Say you'll give him one more chance. The same thing will happen again! It works because switching the cards doesn't mix them. Try it with the cards face up to see.

TRICK OF THE TRADE
The faster you deal, the more fun this trick will be. But don't do it more than twice, as your friend may realize how it works.

Works Every Time!

THERE ARE LOTS of great self-working tricks, but don't be fooled by the name—they may work automatically, but they still require lots of practice. You need to work at each trick until you can perform it smoothly and confidently—perhaps even talking at the same time —otherwise, the trick won't look nearly as impressive.

For self-working tricks, you often need to count in your head as you deal, to make sure you get the number of cards, piles, or rows exactly right.

KEEP IT QUICK

Some self-working tricks involve dealing out stacks of cards again and again, so they can take a long time to perform. Pick short tricks if you can, and never do several together, or you may find your audience loses interest!

MASTER MAGICIAN

PROFESSOR HOFFMANN (1839–1919)

Professor Hoffmann was a lawyer whose real name was Angelo Lewis. He was fascinated by magic, games, and puzzles and wrote several books that tried to list every trick in the world. He used the name Professor Hoffmann because he thought people would not trust him as a lawyer if they knew he was good at trickery! His books include many self-working tricks, which he saw as brain-teasers that were fun to figure out. Many modern self-working tricks come from his books.

BEST FRIENDS STICK TOGETHER

Here's a classic self-working trick. It tells the story of four sets of friends who can't be separated!

1. Go through the deck and take out all the aces, kings, queens, and jacks. Put them in four piles. Say, "The four aces were best friends who always stuck together. So were the kings, the queens, and the jacks."

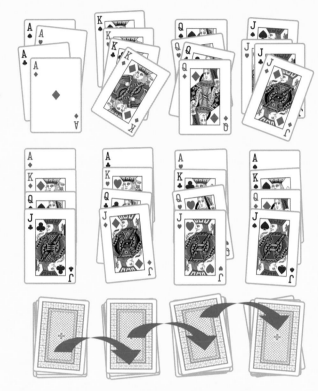

2. Say, "Their teacher was fed up with the four groups of friends talking all the time, so she decided to split them up." Lay out the four aces, deal the four kings on top, then the queens, then the jacks.

3. Turn the four piles face down, pick up the first pile and put it on top of the second. Then pick up the new, bigger pile and put it on top of the third, and then that on the fourth, so you're left with one big pile.

4. Say, "Then, she mixed them even more." Ask a volunteer to **cut** the cards to mix them. This means taking a group of cards off the top, placing them on the table and replacing the rest of the deck on top.

5. Say, "Finally, she divided them into four new groups." Deal the first four cards face down, deal the next four on top, and so on.

6. Say, "But all the friends managed to get back together!" Turn over the piles. All the cards are as they were at the start!

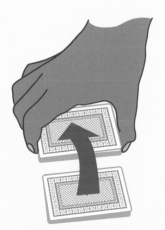

TRICK OF THE TRADE
Add details to the story, or make up something different. Or use made-up science; for example, "Did you know that certain cards are magnetic, and always pull toward each other, even when you try to separate them? Let me show you . . ."

Finding a Card

MANY CARD TRICKS involve asking a volunteer to memorize a card, then magically finding it in the deck. These can be fun, as they get your audience involved. If you use a self-working trick like the one below, it's easy to discover which card your volunteer chose. The key is revealing it in a spectacular way.

THE MIND READER

Before starting this trick, announce that you will correctly guess the card someone chooses, without that person even touching the card. How? Because you're a mind reader!

1. Deal three cards in a row. Deal another overlapping row of three below, and continue until you have seven rows of three cards. Ask a volunteer to memorize any card, then tell you which column it's in.

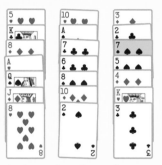

Let's say they choose the seven of spades in the third column.

2. Gather the three columns into one pile, making sure that the column containing their card is the second column you pick up, and so in the middle.

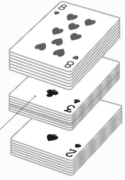

This is the column with the chosen card in it.

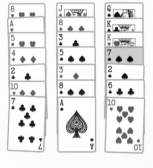

3. Now deal again in the same way—seven rows of three cards—and ask the volunteer to point again to the column with their card. Gather up the cards as before, picking up the chosen column second. **Do this twice more.**

4. When you've dealt for the fourth time, the person's card will always be in the middle of the second column. Gather up the cards again. Theirs is the eleventh card, exactly in the middle of the pile.

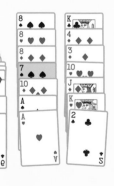

5. Now you know the chosen card, so you can reveal it however you like. You could shuffle the cards, fan them out and pretend to read your volunteer's mind to identify which one is theirs. Another good idea is to use a method called a **force**. Read on to find out how to do this.

FORCING A CARD

You could reveal the chosen card using a force. This means making the volunteer think they can choose any card when in fact you're forcing them to pick one. Here's a simple version of a famous force called the Magician's Choice. You can learn more forces on pages 20–21.

1. After figuring out the chosen card in the Mind Reader trick, spread the 21 cards in a line, face down, and pick out three—the chosen card and two others. Say, "I have a strong feeling that one is your card, but I'm going to let you find your card yourself!"

2. Ask the volunteer to pick any two cards. If they choose the two that aren't their card, say, "OK, let's get rid of these. This is the card you picked. Let's see if it's yours!" Turn it over . . . and of course it is.

3. If the volunteer picks two cards that include their chosen card, say, "OK we'll keep these," and discard the other card instead.

Now ask them to pick one of the two cards left. If they pick the chosen card, say, "So you've picked this one," and turn it over.

If the volunteer picks the card that isn't theirs, say, "OK we'll get rid of that one, which means this must be your card," and turn over the chosen card.

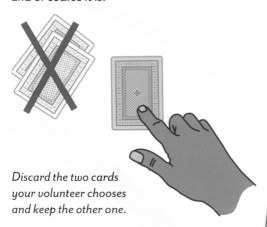

Discard the two cards your volunteer chooses and keep the other one.

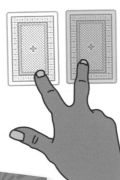

This time, keep the two cards your volunteer chooses and discard the other one.

> **TRICK OF THE TRADE**
> Do this swiftly and with lots of patter, so no one has time to think about the fact that sometimes you keep the cards they pick and sometimes you discard them. Never do it more than once!

MORE MAGICIAN'S CHOICE

This force is even better if you use more cards. For example, deal out all 21 cards into seven piles of three cards, then ask the volunteer to point to four piles.

Use the force above to narrow down the piles to one, then spread out the three cards and use it again. Once again, you'll end up with just the volunteer's card.

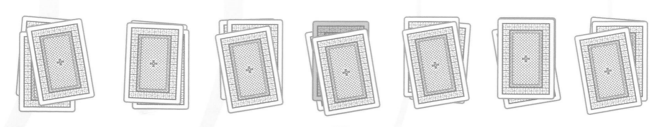

Crafty Cutting

IF YOU'VE TRIED the trick on page 11, you'll know how to cut a deck of cards —divide the deck in two and move the bottom half to the top. This move is handy in card magic because you can do it several times and appear to have mixed up the deck, when in fact the order of the cards never changes!

You can divide a deck anywhere without changing the sequence of the cards.

QUICK PICK

Here's a quick trick that relies on cutting the deck.

1. Sneak a look at the card on the bottom of the deck and remember it.

2. Ask a volunteer to take the top card, look at it, then put it back.

3. Cut the cards several times or ask the volunteer to cut them. Then fan out the cards in your hand. Your volunteer's card will always be the card to the right of the card you memorized.

Your card

Volunteer's card

Great Minds Think Alike

This is a more elaborate version. Before you start, say, "I think we're very alike. In fact, I think if we each had a deck of cards, we'd both pick out exactly the same card!"

TRICK OF THE TRADE
Instead of cutting cards on a table, practice doing it with the deck in your hand. It's quicker, slicker and looks more professional.

1. Put two decks of cards on the table and ask a volunteer to choose a deck and shuffle it. You then shuffle the other deck.

2. Say, "Let's swap decks, so you know you've mixed up mine properly." As you hand over your deck, hold it so you glimpse the bottom card. The volunteer will be concentrating on the deck they're handing to you.

3. Say, "Now let's turn away from each other so there's no cheating. We'll both pick a card from the middle, memorize it, and put it on top." Ignore the card you pick. More importantly, remember the one from the bottom of your deck!

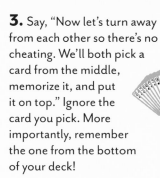

4. Turn back to face each other. Put your deck on the table, cut it, and ask the volunteer to do the same.

5. Say, "I want you to find the card you chose in my deck, and I'll do the same with yours. When you find it, put it face down on the table." Swap decks, then fan the cards and pull out the card to the right of the one you know.

6. Remind the volunteer that you each did exactly the same things. Ask them to take a look at the cards you each chose. They're identical!

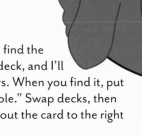

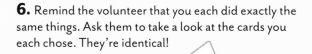

Your card

Volunteer's card

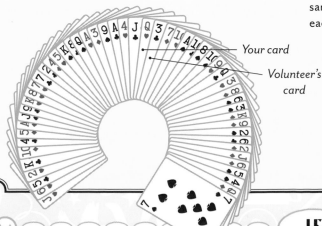

Sneaky Shuffles

SHUFFLING IS AN essential skill. It's a great way of mixing cards—or pretending to mix them when you want to fool your audience. Make sure you can shuffle smoothly and confidently before you start performing. There's nothing worse than dropping your cards in the middle of a trick!

THE STRAIGHT SHUFFLE

For a straight shuffle, hold the deck in your right hand and rest the cards on your left. Lift most of the deck, then drop a few cards in front of and behind the cards in your left hand. Keep going until all the cards are together again. Do this a few times to make sure the cards are mixed up. Do it slowly at first, then speed up once you get the hang of it.

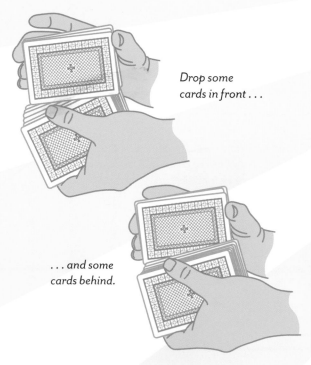

Drop some cards in front . . .

. . . and some cards behind.

FAKING IT

It's easy to keep the bottom card in place using a straight shuffle. Let's say you're doing the Quick Pick trick on page 14. You've sneaked a peek at the bottom card. Now shuffle the cards, but make sure you drop the last few behind the deck in your left hand. The card you know has stayed in the same place, although it looks as if you mixed them up.

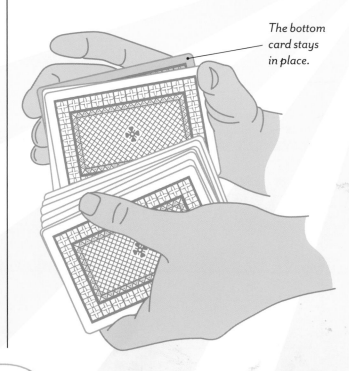

The bottom card stays in place.

MAGIC MOVES

You can also use a straight shuffle to move the bottom card to the top. This can be handy when you want to force a card on a volunteer (see pages 20–21). Imagine you've already looked at the bottom card and done a couple of fake shuffles to keep it at the bottom. Now shuffle the deck again, but this time drop the final card, on its own, on top of the deck. When you then offer the top card to a volunteer, they're taking the one you know.

Move the bottom card to the top.

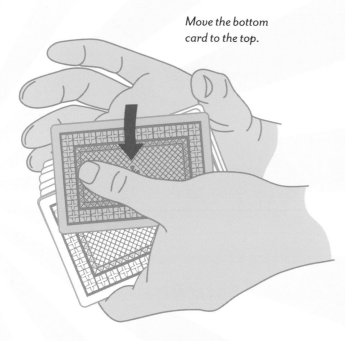

THE RIFFLE SHUFFLE

Magicians often mix cards using a riffle shuffle. It's tricky, but it can look impressive. First, split the deck in half on a table. Using your thumbs, lift a corner of each half, move the halves together and slowly let the cards drop down, overlapping as they fall. Finally, stand the cards on one long edge and push the two halves together.

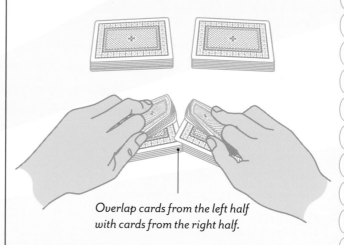

Overlap cards from the left half with cards from the right half.

FAKE RIFFLES

Once you've mastered the riffle shuffle, it's easy to keep the bottom card on the bottom. Split the deck as usual; then, as you riffle the corners of the cards, make sure you drop a few cards from the bottom section of the deck first. Keeping the top card on top is even simpler—just let the last few cards from the top half fall on top. It seems obvious, but remember that your audience doesn't realize you're keeping one card in place, so they won't be looking closely.

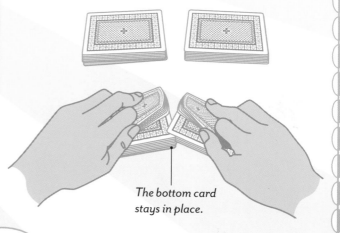

The bottom card stays in place.

Keeping Cards Together

ONCE YOU KNOW how to do false shuffles, you can also try keeping more than one card at the top or bottom of the deck. With lots of practice, you'll be able to keep several cards together, even if you appear to shuffle the deck a few times. This means you can try even more impressive tricks.

THE SECRET OF DEALING

The Amazing Aces trick on the next page works because you reverse the order of a pile when you deal it out. This means that the aces that started on top were moved to the bottom of the pile the volunteer dealt—so they ended up back on top when the pile was dealt again. This method is used a lot in card magic. Turn to pages 20–21 to find more dealing tips.

MASTER MAGICIAN

JEAN HUGARD (1872–1959)   FRED BRAUE (1906–1962)

Amazing Aces is a very famous, old trick that was invented by two magicians named Jean Hugard and Fred Braue. Jean Hugard was a well-known Australian magician who performed many entertaining stage shows, sometimes dressed as a mysterious Chinese man called Chin Sun Loo. In the 1920s he had his own magic theater in Luna Park, a famous amusement park at Coney Island in New York. After retiring, he wrote many magic books with Fred Braue, who was a journalist and expert on card tricks. They compiled hundreds of card tricks, including all kinds of complicated false shuffles.

Luna Park, Surf Avenue, Coney Island, N.Y.

The entrance to Luna Park, Coney Island, in 1913.

AMAZING ACES

In this trick, a volunteer deals out piles of cards at random, but finds that there's an ace on top of each pile! The secret is to make sure the four aces are on the top of the deck before you start.

1. First, take out a deck of cards that has the four aces on top. Introduce the trick, saying, "Magicians are always pulling aces out of a deck, but I think you could do it yourself, without my help." As you talk, do a false riffle shuffle, so no one will suspect that you've set up the deck.

2. Hand the deck to a volunteer and ask them to start dealing cards into a pile, face down. Tell them they can stop whenever they like. Make it clear that it's their choice how many to deal.

3. Now ask the volunteer to pick up the cards and deal them into four piles. Move away or turn your back to make it clear you can't touch the cards.

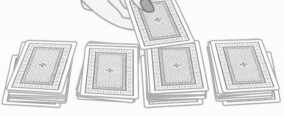

4. Remind the volunteer that you think they can magically find the aces. Ask them to turn over the top card of each pile. They're all aces!

TRICK OF THE TRADE
When you use this trick in a show, do it after Best Friends Stick Together (page 11). Gather up the four aces last and put them on top of the deck, then you're ready!

Dodgy Dealing

DEALING OUT a pile of cards looks straightforward, but for magicians or cheating card players, it can be a good way of making cards end up where you want them. As you've already seen, accurate dealing is an essential part of many self-working tricks. It's also a good way of forcing a card.

DEALING TO FORCE

Here's how to use dealing to make someone pick the top card, while they think they're choosing one at random from the deck.

Although experts can deal very fast, don't be tempted to throw the cards down too quickly—they may flip over, ruining your trick.

Give me a number between one and ten.

Five!

So now I need you to deal five cards face down, like this, then look at and memorize the fifth card.

1. Make sure you know the top card and do a false shuffle to keep it there, or peek at the bottom card and move it to the top with a false shuffle (see pages 16–17). Then ask a volunteer to say a number between one and ten. If they choose five, for example, ask them to deal five cards face down then look at and memorize the fifth card. As you talk, demonstrate by dealing five cards face down.

This is the card you know, from the top of the pack.

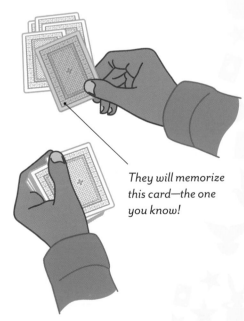

They will memorize this card—the one you know!

2. Put the pile you dealt back on the top of the deck. Now ask the volunteer to deal out their five cards. Because you've just reversed the order by dealing them, the card you know is now the fifth one.

DEALING FROM THE BOTTOM

Another sneaky dealing trick is to peek at the bottom card of the deck and do a few false shuffles to keep it in place. While you shuffle, say, "Maybe you think I can fix the cards on top of the deck—so instead I'll deal from the bottom."

Ask a volunteer to say a number between one and 52. Explain you'll deal cards until you come to their number, then they can memorize that card. The key is to push back the bottom card slightly as you talk. When you deal, pull out the next to bottom card each time—until you come to the number they chose, when you deal the bottom card.

Push the bottom card back slightly so you do not pull it out until you're ready.

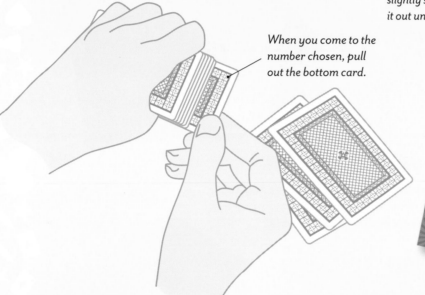

When you come to the number chosen, pull out the bottom card.

TRICK OF THE TRADE
Once you've forced the card, ask the volunteer to shuffle the deck as much as they like, or spread the cards on the table to mix them up. It doesn't matter what they do—you'll still be able to identify their card.

MASTER MAGICIAN

DAI VERNON (1894–1992)

*Dai Vernon was a Canadian **conjuror** who became fascinated with card tricks after seeing a magic show when he was seven. He had a long career in magic and was so skilled that other magicians still call him the Professor. He was also famous for being the only person to fool the magician Harry Houdini, who boasted that he could always figure out how tricks were done.*

Vernon was an expert in dealing from the top and bottom of the deck to force cards. He heard rumors about a gambler named Allen Kennedy who could secretly order the cards so he could deal a winning hand of cards from the middle of the deck. Desperate to know how it was done, Vernon tracked down Kennedy and learned the fiendishly hard sleight from him. He kept the method a secret!

Is THIS Your Card?

NOW YOU KNOW how to force a card on an unsuspecting volunteer, and how to make sure that the card ends up on the top or bottom of the deck. Next comes your big moment—revealing the person's card. You could just pull it out of the pack . . . or you could try one of these daring and dramatic methods that will leave your audience amazed.

THE JUMPING CARD

This method of revealing the top card is quite simple, but don't tell the audience what you're about to do—then they'll get a shock when you suddenly smack the cards down on the table!

1. Hold the deck in your right hand. Use your left hand to secretly push the top card a little way to the right. Your right hand should cover up what you're doing. Keep talking so no one looks too closely.

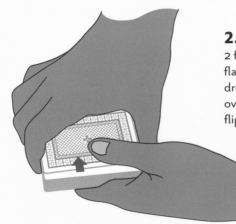

2. Hold the deck about 2 feet (60 cm) above a flat surface, then suddenly drop it straight down. The overhanging top card will flip over and fall face-up.

3. Don't panic if the top card shoots off to the side, or the deck lands in a mess. The top card should still be separated from the rest. If cards go everywhere, then just find the card, pull it out, and pretend you meant that to happen!

SLAP BANG!

Here's a funny, messy way of revealing the card on the bottom of the deck.

1. Ask the volunteer to hold the deck firmly, like this.

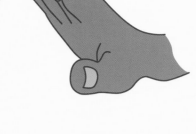

Bottom card

2. Sharply slap the end of the deck a few times to make cards fall out. The bottom card will be the last card left in the person's hand.

AMAZING BRAIN POWER

If the chosen card is on the top of the deck, say you'll use your amazing brain power to find it.

1. First, wet your lips and press them against the deck. You could do this sneakily, or say you're kissing the cards for luck.

2. Press the deck against your forehead so that the top card sticks to it. Say, "My brain power is burning through the cards. I'm getting something." Then remove the deck to leave the chosen card stuck to your forehead.

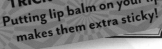

TRICK OF THE TRADE
Putting lip balm on your lips makes them extra sticky!

MASTER MAGICIAN

HERBERT MILTON
(1897–1960)

Herbert Milton was a card magician who invented a way of revealing a card with his foot. He asked a volunteer to put the deck on the floor, cut it and look at the top card, then put the two piles back together. He then nudged the deck with his foot and it parted exactly where the volunteer cut it. Can you figure out how he did it? See page 32 for the answer.

Perfect Props

FOR MOST CARD tricks, the only equipment you need is a deck of cards. However, you might want to add a few extra props if you're putting on a performance, just to give your act variety. Choose carefully—too many props can get in the way and overshadow your card skills.

You can buy expensive magic props, but it's easier to use everyday objects. For example, try writing the name of a card you're going to force and seal it in an envelope.

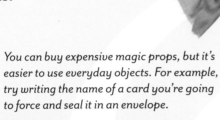

LANCE BURTON (born 1960)

Lance Burton is a popular and skilled American magician who has an extravagant stage show in Las Vegas. Although his act often uses complicated props and glamorous costumes, he also does simple card tricks that seem more amazing because they look so effortless. For example, he invented a trick in which the only prop is the ordinary suit he's wearing. He asks a volunteer to shuffle a deck of cards and place them in the inside pocket of his jacket, first checking that the pocket is empty. He then reaches into the jacket and pulls out four aces from the deck without even looking at them. Can you guess how he does the trick? See page 32 for the answer.

MAGIC CLOCK

This trick uses one simple prop: a piece of cardboard or thick paper. Remember to use lots of acting to make your revelations seem impressive.

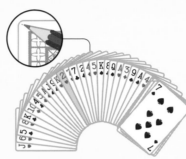

Front

Back

YOU WILL CHOOSE THE TWO OF HEARTS

Make sure the writing doesn't show through on the clock side.

1. Before you show the trick, draw a clock face on one side of the paper. Now choose a card—for example, the two of hearts—and write it as a prediction on the other side of the paper, like this.

2. Now find the two of hearts and put a tiny pencil mark in one corner on the back, just enough for you to see. Put the card in the thirteenth position from the top of the deck.

3. Tell your audience you have a magic clock. Put the paper on the table, without showing the writing underneath. You could also give the cards a quick false riffle, leaving a large chunk unmixed on top. Now ask a volunteer to think of a number from the clock. Turn your back and tell them to deal out that number of cards from the top of the deck and keep them.

Let's say they chose the number five.

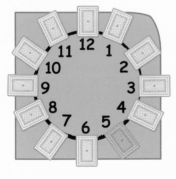

4. Say, "Now the clock will tell me the number you chose." Deal 12 cards into a pile, counting as you go. Now take that pile and deal them out beside the clock numbers, from 1 to 12. Watch out for your secretly marked card. It will be beside the number they chose.

5. Announce the person's number with lots of drama.

The clock is telling me the number . . . five!

6. Ask the person to peek at the card in the fifth position and replace it. This time, pretend the clock is telling you the name of the card.

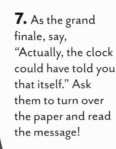

I think the card is . . . the two of hearts!

7. As the grand finale, say, "Actually, the clock could have told you that itself." Ask them to turn over the paper and read the message!

TRICK OF THE TRADE
Don't take too long between steps 5, 6, and 7—the surprises need to keep coming to leave your volunteer really baffled.

Tough Stuff

PROFESSIONAL MAGICIANS DO all kinds of amazing sleights, which are difficult for beginners. Once you've mastered the basic sleights in this book, such as false shuffles and bottom dealing, try a few trickier ones. But don't worry if you don't get the hang of them right away. Remember, it's best to perform one perfect sleight than lots of clumsy ones!

The Double Lift

One famous sleight is the double lift. The magician appears to turn over the top card of a deck when actually lifting two cards. The key is separating the top two cards from the rest of the deck.

One way of doing this is to fan through the cards quickly, as if you're checking they're all face down, then sneak the little finger of your left hand just under the second card, creating a small gap. Put your right hand over the top of the deck to cover this.

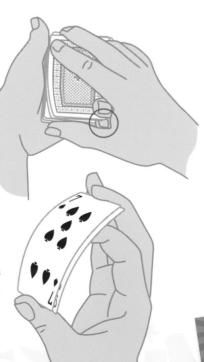

Now take hold of the two cards firmly with your right hand and lift them up as if you're displaying the top card. The goal is to make the double lift look as smooth and casual as lifting just one card.

The Rising Card

A great way of using a double lift in a trick is to make a card seem to rise from the middle to the top of the deck.

1. While you introduce the trick, shuffle the cards then separate the top two. Do a double lift to show the "top" card. Say, "Remember the top card—the five of clubs."

2. Replace the cards on top of the deck. Say, "Let's move the five of clubs further down the deck." Take just the top card and push it into the middle of the deck.

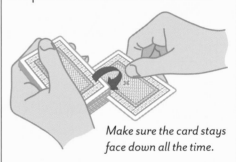

Make sure the card stays face down all the time.

3. Say, "But if I want it back, I just snap my fingers," (or tap the deck, or some other gesture) "and the card rises through the deck to the top." Turn over the top card—the five of clubs is back!

TRICK OF THE TRADE

Whether you're lifting one or two cards, make sure you always do it in the same way. Your audience will soon get suspicious if your hands are in a different position when you do a double lift!

DAVID BLAINE (born 1973)

David Blaine is an American **illusionist** who is famous for high-profile stunts, but also for his amazing close-up sleights, which he often performs in the street. He is an expert at double and even triple lifts, and makes the moves so smoothly that people are astounded by the way he appears to make cards move, vanish, and reappear.

It's the ultimate goal of magicians—to make the audience believe something is magic, even though they know there must be a trick somewhere.

David Blaine performs card tricks for a group of students.

NOW YOU SEE IT . . .

Back palming involves flipping a card onto the back of a hand to hide it, then flicking it forward to make it reappear. Here's the secret.

1. Hold the card out to your side like this, facing the audience.

2. Now bend your fingers over to make a fist, with your first and little fingers holding onto the long edges of the card.

3. Lift up your thumb and stretch out your fingers so that you're holding the card behind your hand. The corners of the card won't be visible from a distance.

To make the card reappear, reverse the process. Now practice until you can do each flick in the blink of an eye!

PALMING CARDS

Master magicians often use a technique called palming. This involves making a card "disappear" by hiding it in the palm of their hand and keeping it turned away from the audience. It's very difficult if you have small hands!

Show Time!

WHEN YOU CAN do a few card tricks flawlessly, it's time to impress your friends, family, and maybe even complete strangers. Card tricks are ideal for short, one-off performances while you're having lunch at school or waiting for a bus. If you want to put on a complete magic show, here are some tips.

PLAN IT OUT

Plan your act very carefully, bearing in mind who your audience is and what they will enjoy. Start with a quick trick to grab their attention, end with something spectacular, and don't try to cram in too much, or people may start getting bored. Work out your patter and rehearse it. Being a magician is like acting in a play. If you know your lines and moves perfectly, you're less likely to feel nervous.

The magician Harry Houdini started his career by calling himself King of Cards. Why not give yourself a stage name too, and make posters like Houdini's to advertise your show?

MASTER MAGICIAN

CARDINI (1895–1973)

Cardini was a Welsh magician. He created one of the best magic shows ever, using great acting and lots of imagination. Dressed in an elegant dinner suit and white gloves, he acted the role of a befuddled gentleman who seemed amazed and confused every time he made magic happen. For example, he would try to remove his gloves, only for fans of cards to keep appearing at his fingertips, falling to the stage around him. He didn't speak at all, but instead used music, making cards, silk scarves, and other small props appear or disappear perfectly in time with the music. Audiences had never seen an act like it, and Cardini became an extremely successful magician.

SUIT YOUR STYLE

Remember that tricks are only part of the show—you need to put on a memorable performance, too. The key is to do what you're good at. If you like to crack jokes, work some into your patter, or try a bit of **slapstick** comedy with an assistant or a puppet. If you'd rather stay serious, try pretending you're a mysterious, cloaked wizard. Use costumes, makeup, lighting, and background music to make the effect more impressive.

TRICK OF THE TRADE
Never reveal the secrets behind your tricks, no matter how much people beg you to tell them. You'll ruin the illusion you create and may leave your audience feeling disappointed about how simple the tricks were!

Here are a few ideas to start you thinking about exciting costumes and characters.

Go for a traditional look by dressing in a classic magician's outfit of top hat, dress clothes, and a long, flowing cloak. It will help you look professional.

Wear a bold, bizarre costume with a crazy wig and maybe even face paint or body glitter to help you grab your audience's attention!

Try creating a mysterious, masked character dressed head to toe in black. Act as if you have strange mental powers that make magic happen.

DON'T PANIC!

If you make a mistake—for example, you deal the wrong cards—then start again if you can, pretending it's all part of a complicated build-up. If the trick is completely ruined—say a hidden card drops out of your pocket—move on to the next trick fast.

Never stop, appear flustered, or apologize. Remember, you're an actor playing a role. If you're really entertaining and the audience likes you, they may not mind too much. If you're able to make a joke of it, they might even wonder if it's part of the act.

Glossary

anagram
a word or phrase that is made by rearranging the letters of another word or phrase

conjuror
another word for magician; traditionally, conjurors perform tricks such as making things appear or disappear.

con man
short for confidence man; someone who appears to be honest, but really cheats people out of money

cut
to take a chunk of cards from the top of a face-down pile, put them on the table, then pick up the rest of the pile and place it on top of the cut section

dealer
the person who deals, or hands out, cards from the deck as part of a card game

force
a method of appearing to offer a volunteer a random choice of card when, in fact, you are making sure they pick the one you want them to have

illusionist
another word for magician; illusionists often perform large-scale magic tricks that create impossible or spooky effects, such as objects floating or someone being sawn in half.

joker
a card that usually has a picture of a jester on it; jokers are used in some card games. They can also be used to replace lost or damaged cards.

misdirect
to deliberately draw an audience's attention away from something you don't want them to see or think too much about

patter
prepared, practiced speech that magicians use when performing magic tricks

prop
short for property; any object that is used to help perform a trick

shuffle
to mix up a deck of cards in your hands; you usually shuffle the deck several times to make sure the cards are properly mixed. A false shuffle is a way of pretending to mix the deck when really keeping certain cards in place.

slapstick
silly, funny, and over-the-top; clowns often perform slapstick comedy. Pretending to slip on banana peels is an example.

sleight-of-hand; sleight
A sleight (pronounced slight) is the technique of secretly moving or swapping cards to create a magical effect.

Web Sites

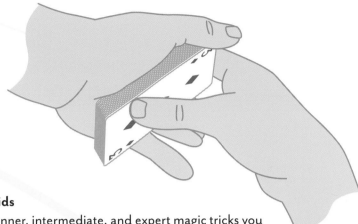

Activity TV – Magic Tricks For Kids
www.activitytv.com/magic-tricks-for-kids
Watch videos and print out steps for beginner, intermediate, and expert magic tricks you can do to amaze your friends.

Card Sleights
www.sharkmagic.com/blog/category/card-sleights
Watch a clear video that takes you through the stages of doing a double lift, with lots of useful hints and tips.

MagicianSchool.com – Famous Magician Biographies
www.magicianschool.com/biographies.php
Read about the lives of famous professional magicians including Harry Houdini, David Copperfield, and Lance Burton.

MagicPedia
www.geniimagazine.com/wiki/index.php/Main_Page
Discover hundreds of articles about famous magicians and clever trick techniques, all written by magic enthusiasts.

The Society of American Magicians
www.magicsam.com
Learn about the prestigious society formed in 1902 to help promote the ideals and ethics of magicians around the world.

The Society of Young Magicians
www.magicsym.com
Learn about the Society of Young Magicians, a group formed by the Society of American Magicians. Join the S.Y.M. to get newsletters featuring tips and articles by magicians from across the country.

Index

SECRETS OF MAGIC . . . REVEALED!

Page 23 How did Herbert Milton reveal a card with his foot?

Answer: When the volunteer had looked at a card and put it back down, Herbert Milton pointed at it and told the person to replace the top half of the deck on top. As he pointed, he sneakily dropped a few grains of salt on top of the chosen card. When he kicked the cards, the salt grains acted like ball bearings and made the top half of the deck roll to one side.

Page 24 How did Lance Burton pull four aces from a deck of cards in his pocket?

Answer: Before the show, he took the four aces out of the deck and put them in the breast pocket of his shirt—so when he appeared to be reaching into his jacket pocket, he was pulling the aces out of his shirt pocket instead.